the best of...
massive attack

the best of...
massive attack

Wise Publications
part of The Music Sales Group

London / New York / Paris / Sydney / Copenhagen / Berlin / Madrid / Tokyo

Published by:
Wise Publications
8/9 Frith Street, London W1D 3JB, England.

Exclusive distributors:
Music Sales Limited
Distribution Centre, Newmarket Road,
Bury St. Edmunds Suffolk IP33 3YB, England.
Music Sales Pty Limited
120 Rothschild Avenue, Rosebery, NSW 2018, Australia.

Order No. AM977251
ISBN 1-84449-041-6
This book © Copyright 2003 by Wise Publications.

Compiled by Nick Crispin.
Music arrangements by Derek Jones.
Music processed by Paul Ewers Music Design.

Printed in the United Kingdom by Thanet Press Limited.

www.musicsales.com

angel 6

be thankful for what you've got 18

better things 12

black milk 23

future proof 28

hymn of the big wheel 34

lately 40

man next door 84

name taken 46

one love 52

a prayer for england 58

protection 66

risingson 74

safe from harm 89

sly 96

special cases 100

teardrop 104

unfinished sympathy 110

weather storm 122

what your soul sings 116

angel

Words & Music by Robert Del Naja,
Grantley Marshall, Andrew Vowles & Horace Andy

You_____ are my__ an - gel._____

Come from way a-bove___ to bring me love.___

Her eyes,___ she's on the

N.C.

dark side.

Neu-tral-ize

ev-'ry man in sight.

Love you, love you, love you, love you, love you, love you, love you, love you,

Cm

love you, love you, love you, love you, love you, love you, love you, love you,

9

Repeat ad lib. to fade

11

better things

**Words & Music by Tracey Thorn, Benjamin Watt,
Andrew Vowles, Robert Del Naja, Grantley Marshall & James Brown**

Percussion

Perc. cont. sim.

Hear me say, bet- ter things will sure - ly come_ my way._

Percussion

be thankful for what you've got

Words & Music by William De Vaughn

Though you___ may

not drive a great big Ca - dil - lac, gang - ster white - walls, T. V. an - ten - nae in the back. You may not have a car at all.

black milk

Words & Music by Robert Del Naja, Grantley Marshall, Andrew Vowles, Elizabeth Fraser & Manfred Mann

1. You're not__ my eat - er.__
2. Eat me__ in the space_____
3. The most__ lev - el__

Mo - ther____ foun - tain,____

or live____ or not____ at____ all.____

All's   there___   to   love._____

26

On - ly___ love.___

Repeat 4 times ad lib.

F#m

Repeat ad lib. to fade

F#m

27

future proof

Words & Music by Robert Del Naja & Neil Davidge

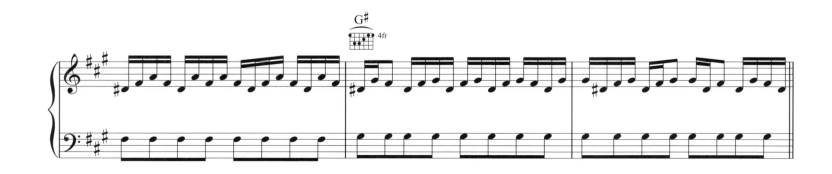

Real   thin__   air.___

hymn of the big wheel

Words & Music by Robert Del Naja, Andrew Vowles, Grantley Marshall, Horace Andy & Neneh Cherry

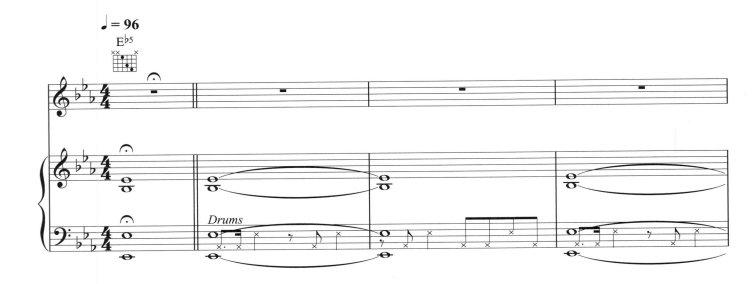

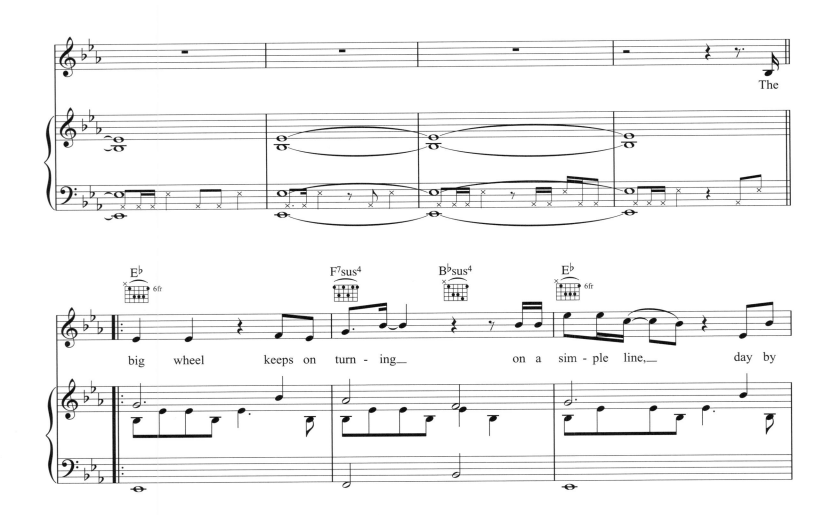

day.

The earth spins on it's ax - is.

One man strug - gle while a - no - ther re - lax - es.

1. There's a
2. We

hole in my soul like a ca - vi - ty, seems like the world___ is out to ga - ther just by
sang a - bout the sun and dance a - mong the trees and we list - ened to the whis - per of the
3. Childs si - lent prayers my hope___ hides in dis - guise while sa - tel - lites and cam - eras watch

gra - vi - ty.___ The wheel keeps turn - ing, the sky's re - ar - ran - ging,
ci - ty on the breeze. Will you cry the most in a lead free zone,
from the skies. An ac - id drop of rain re - cy - cled from the___ sea. It

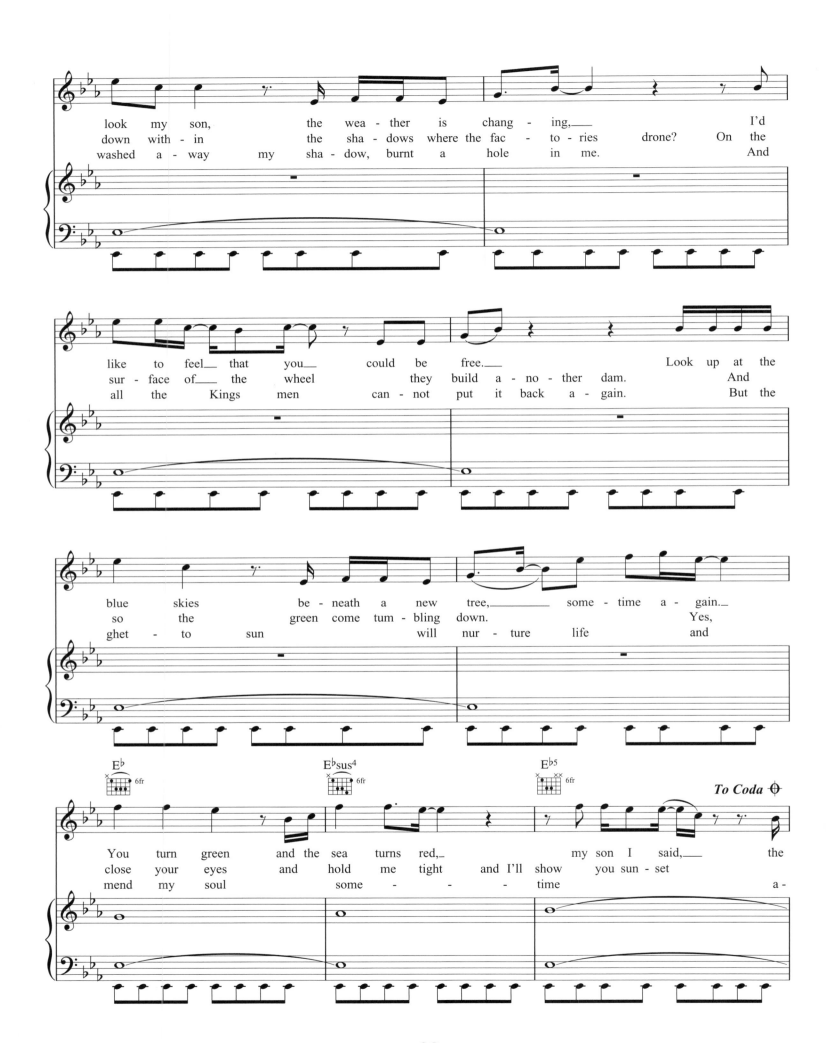

lately

Words & Music by Larry Brownlee, Gus Redmond, Jeffrey Simon, Fred Simon, Grantley Marshall, Andrew Vowles & Robert Del Naja

I used to syn-chro-nise it with your bo - dy. Mak-ing it so

tight nev-er let-ting go.____ I used to syn-chro-nise it with your bo-

Repeat ad lib. to fade

45

name taken

Words & Music by Robert Del Naja & Neil Davidge

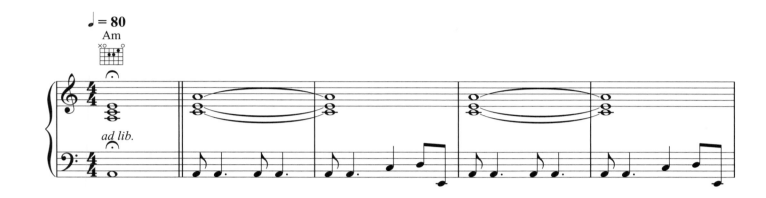

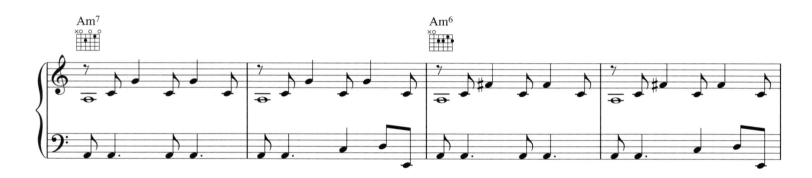

Op - en rooms, Peel a - way con - tra - zoom. chil - dren play.

To Coda ⊕

Pic - tures may, fa - ces may.

48

And fade a - way._____

Repeat ad lib. to fade

one love

**Words & Music by Robert Del Naja, Grantley Marshall,
Andrew Vowles, Horace Andy & J.C. Williams**

- ev - er._____
charm._____
things seem._____

You I love____ and not an - oth - er
They say don't lay your eggs in one
Ev - er so faith - ful, ev - er so sure.____

- oth - er._____
bas - ket._____
_____

And I know we'll al - ways be to -
If the bas - ket should fall all the eggs will be
No man could ev - er ask for more.____

To Coda ⊕

- ge - ther._____
bro - ken._____
_____ hear me now.

Some men have one love,____ two and
But I be - lieve____ in

three love._____
one love._____

Four and five____ and
I be - lieve____ in

53

I be - lieve___ in one love.

I be - lieve,___ yeah,_____ oh, yeah,___ in

one love, in one love, in

one love, in one love. I be -

a prayer for england

Words & Music by Sinead O'Connor, Robert Del Naja & Neil Davidge

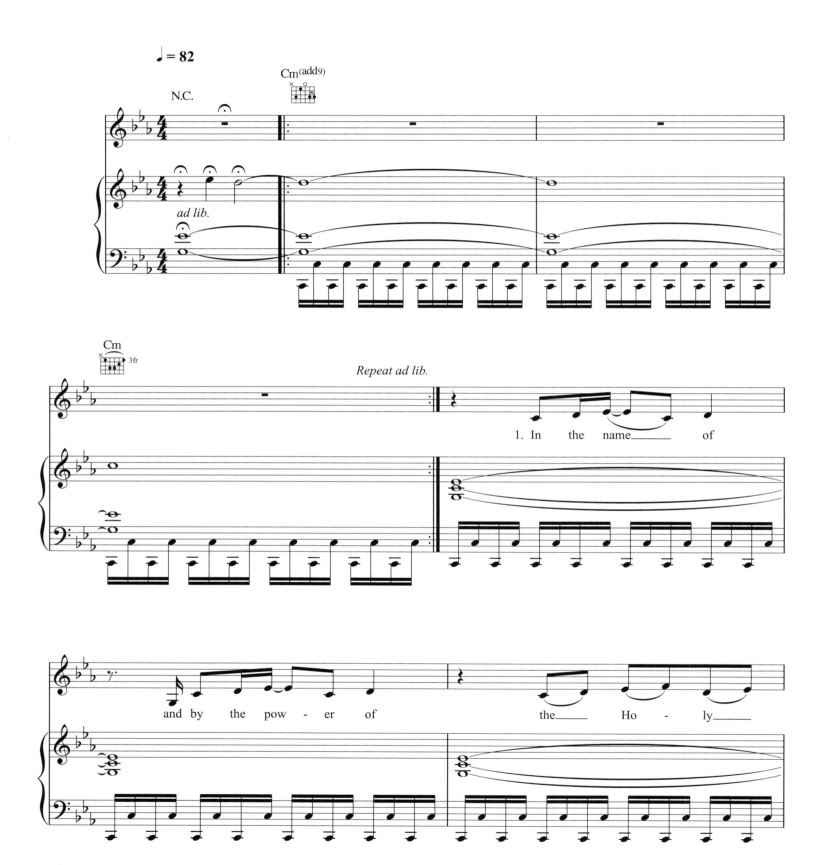

Spi - - rit may we in - voke your
in - ter - ces - sion for the_____ chil - dren of
Eng - land. Some of whom have_____ seen_____
mur - der so ob - scene,_____ some of whom have been_____

Gm⁷/C

Cm

59

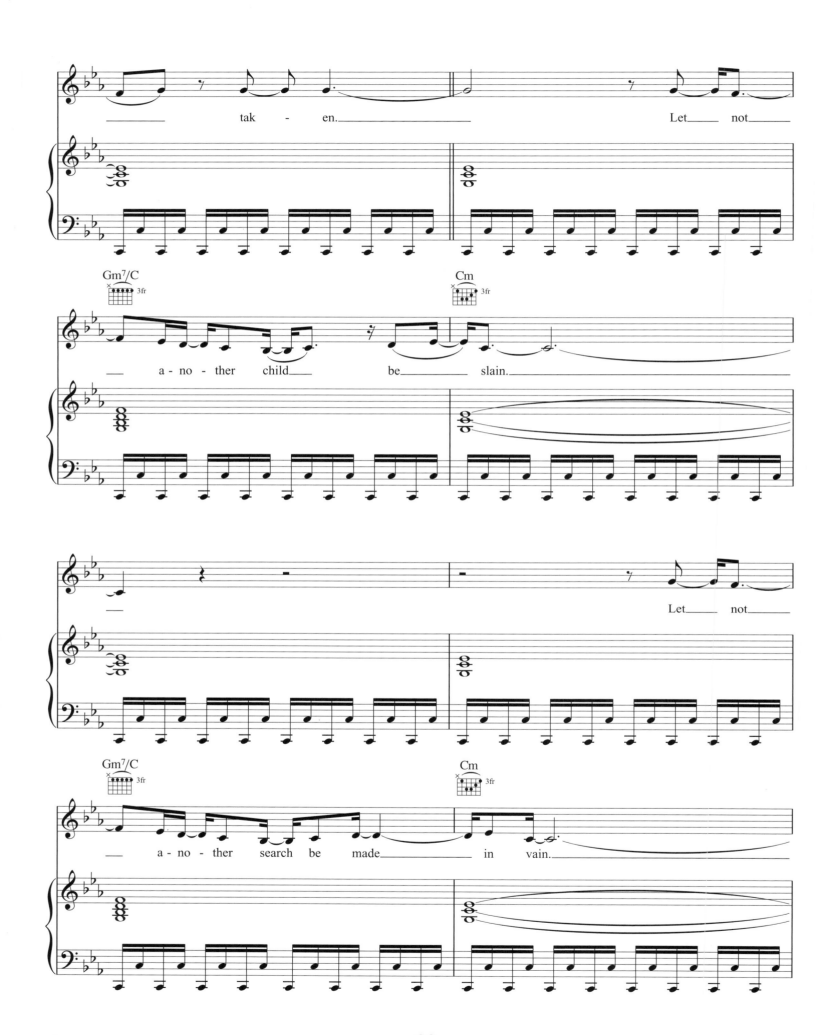

Jah__ calls the ones__ whose be - liefs kill chil - dren too.

Feel the love of__ you and__ be healed.

And__ may we all cry__ too_____ for rep - re - sent - ing__ you

D.S. al Coda

__ so bad - ly,_____ so bad - ly.

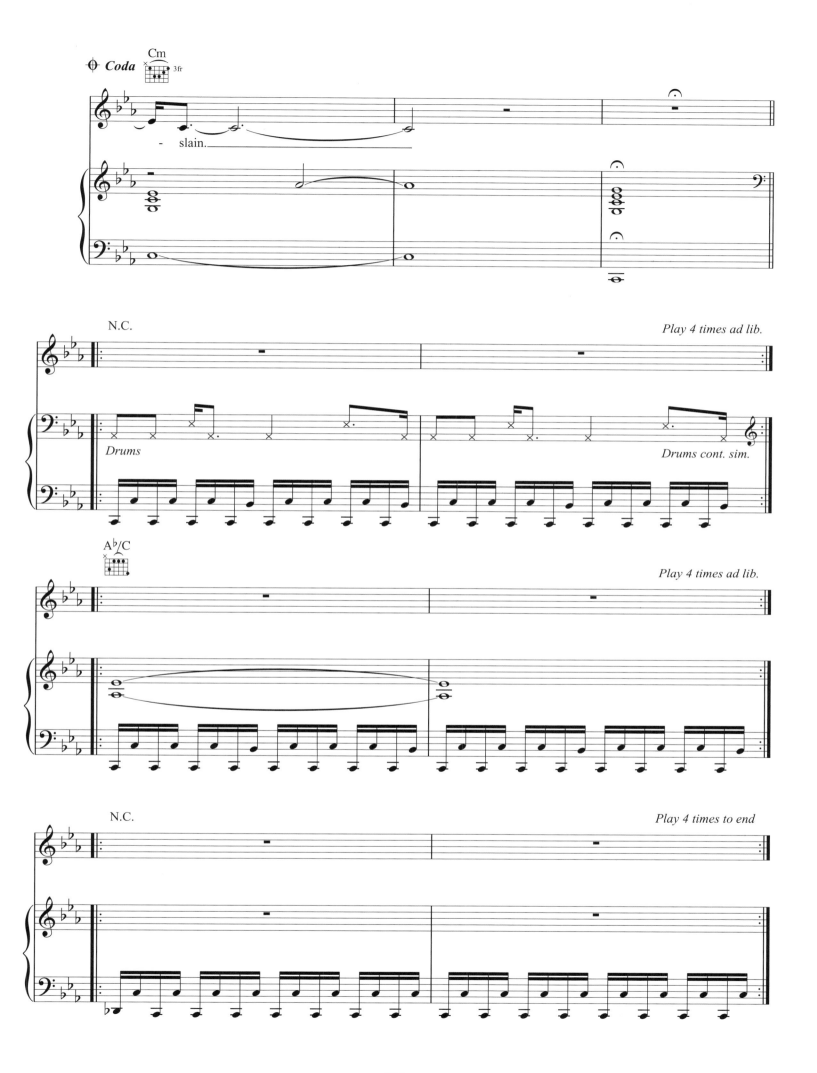

protection

Words & Music by Tracey Thorn, Andrew Vowles, Robert Del Naja & Grantley Marshall

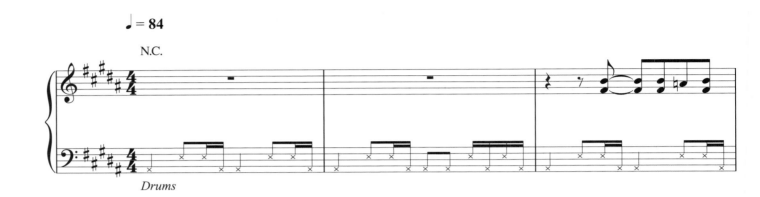

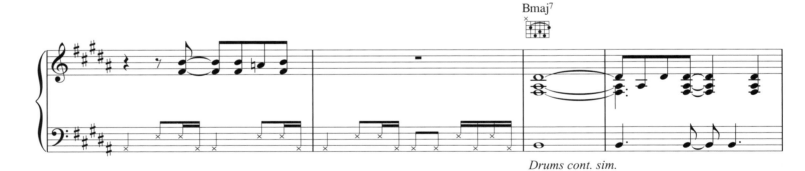

70

risingson

**Words & Music by Andrew Vowles, Robert De Naja,
Grantley Marshall, Lou Reed & Pete Seeger**

you lick a shine up-on your fore-head or___ check it by the signs in the cor-ri-dor.___

You light my ways___ through the club maze, we would strug-gle through the dub daze.

Drums cont. sim.

(Ah.)___

I see my-self in there up-on my lov-er,___ it's how you go down to the men's room sink,___

Why you wan - na take me to this par - ty and breathe?_ I'm dy - ing to leave._ Ev - 'ry

Drums

time we grind we know we sev - ered lines.

Drums cont. sim.

Where have all those flow - ers gone,_ long time pass - ing.

Drums

Why you keep me test - ing, keep me task - ing. You keep on ask - ing._

Drums cont. sim.

Toy - like peo - ple make me boy - like. Toy - like peo - ple make me boy - like. They're in -

vi - si - ble, when the trip it flips,_ they get phy - si - cal, way be - low my lips._ And ev - 'ry -

thing you got, hoi - pol - loi like. Now you're lost and you're le - thal. And

now's a - bout the time you got - ta leave all these good peo - ple. (Dream

Drums

Drums cont. sim.

on.)

(Ah.)

(Ah.)

Ni - cer than the bird up in the tree - top,

cheap - er than the chip in - side my lap - top.

All the va - ri - a - tions you could do with me,__

ni - cer than the girl up in a mind you free.__ Au - to - ma - tic cry - stal re - mote con - trol.__

They come to move your soul.__ You're gon - na fade in - to the back - ground.

Like a bet - ter smoke - 'll bring you back round. Like a man slide__ in - side you my dear.__

Your cheep beer's filled with cro - co - dile tears. See 'em run now you've gone. (Dream

man next door

Words & Music by John Holt

I've got to get a-way from here,_____ this is not a_

_ place for_ me to stay. I've got to take my_ fa - mi - ly_____

and_ find a qui - et place._____

place.

Drip, drip, drip, drip, drip, drip, drip, drip.

Drip, drip, drip, drip, drip, drip, drip, drip.

safe from harm

***Words & Music by Robert Del Naja, Grantley Marshall,
Andrew Vowles, Shara Nelson & Billy Cobham***

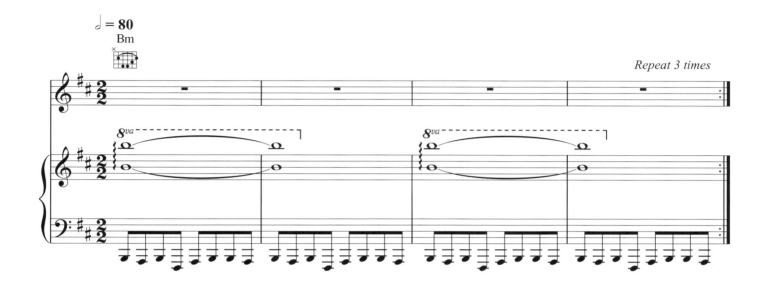

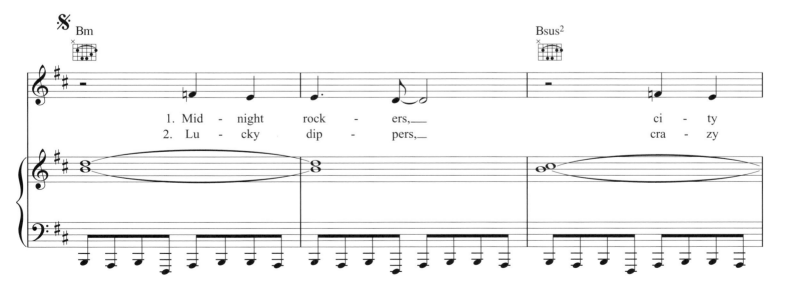

1. Mid - night rock - ers,___ ci - ty
2. Lu - cky dip - pers,___ cra - zy

To Coda ⊕

Ter - ro - rists in - fec - tious and dan - ger - ous. Friends and e - ne - mies are far - thest con - tai -

- ger - ous. I was look - in' back to see if you were look - in' back at me to

see me look - in' back at you.

D.S. al Coda

Coda

Bm

Te - te - te - te ter - ro - rists in - fec - tious and dan -

Bsus²

- ger - ous. Friends and e - ne - mies are far - thest con - tai - ger - ous. And they

sly

**Words & Music by Nicolette Suwoton, Robert Del Naja,
Andrew Vowles, Grantley Marshall, Nellee Hooper & Vivian Goldman**

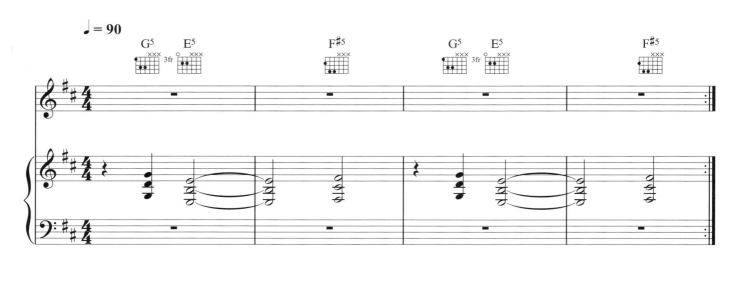

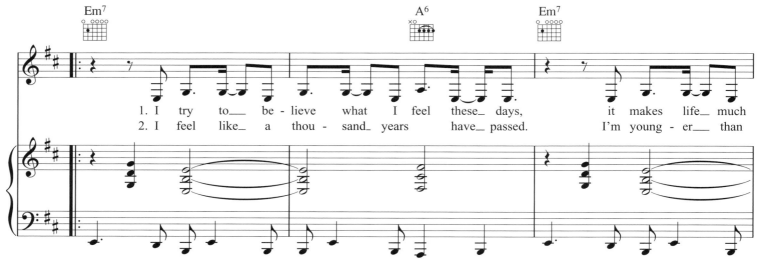

1. I try to___ be - lieve what I feel these___ days, it makes life___ much
2. I feel like___ a thou - sand___ years have___ passed. I'm young - er___ than

ea - sier for me.   It's hard to___ de - cide what___ is real these___ days
I used to be.   I feel like___ the world is___ my home at___ last,

special cases

Words & Music by Sinead O'Connor, Robert Del Naja & Neil Davidge

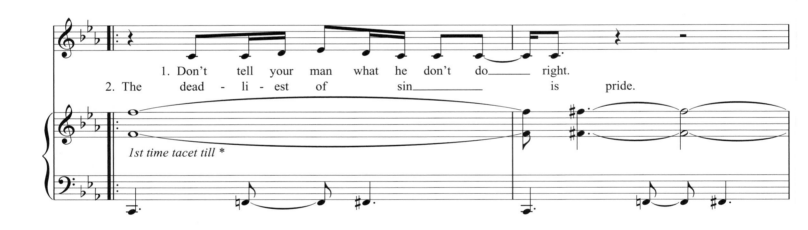

1. Don't tell your man what he don't do right.
2. The deadliest of sin is pride.

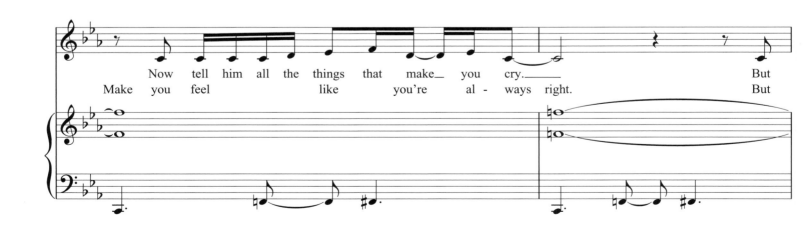

Now tell him all the things that make you cry. But
Make you feel like you're always right. But

1st time tacet till *

check your-self___ for your own___ shit, and
there are al - ways two___ sides. It takes

don't be mak - ing out like it's all___ his.
two to make___ love, two to make a life.

Take a look a round the world.___ You see such bad things hap - pen - ing.___
Take a look a round the world.___ You see such mad things hap - pen - ing.___

There are ma - ny good___ men,___
There are few___ good___ men,___

ask your - self___ is he one of them?
thank your luck - y stars that he's one of them.

1.

2.

103

teardrop

**Words & Music by Robert Del Naja, Grantley Marshall,
Andrew Vowles & Elizabeth Fraser**

Verse 3:
Water is my eye
Most faithful mirror
Fearless on my breath.
Teardrop on the fire
Of a confession
Fearless on my breath.
Most faithful mirror
Fearless on my breath.

unfinished sympathy

Words & Music by Robert Del Naja, Grantley Marshall, Andrew Vowles, Shara Nelson & Jonathan Sharp

1. I know_ that I've_ i - ma - gined love_ be - fore_
(Verse 2 see block lyric)

and how_ it could_ be with_ you._

Real - ly hurt_ me ba - by, real - ly hurt_ me ba - by.

How can you have_ a day_ with - out_ a night?_

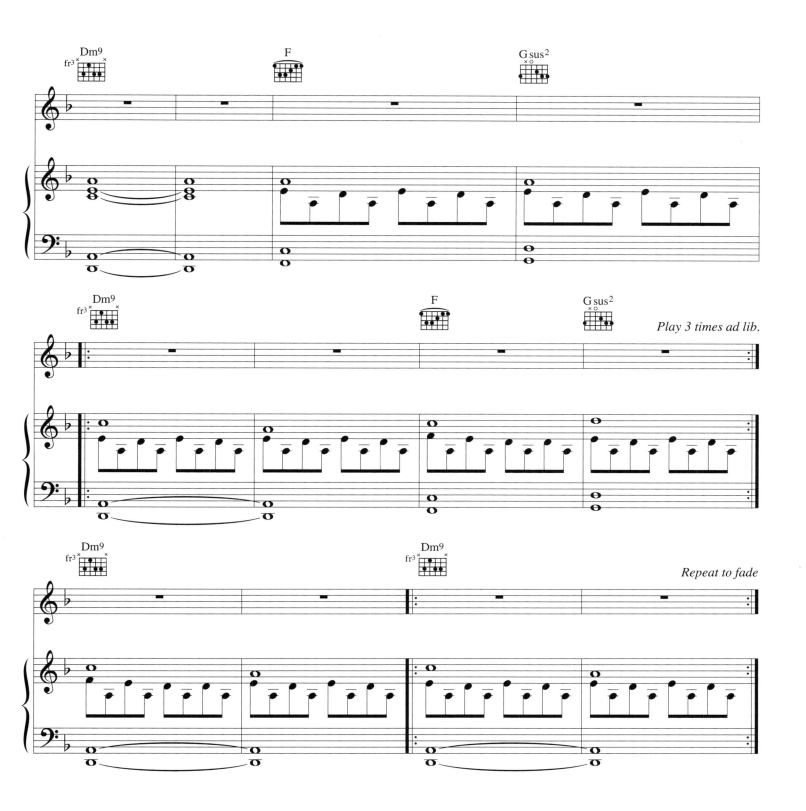

Verse 2:
The curiousness of your potential kiss
Has got my mind and body aching
Really hurt me baby
Really hurt me baby
How can you have a day without a night?
You're the book that I have opened
And now I've got to know much more.

what your soul sings

Words & Music by Sinead O'Connor, Robert Del Naja & Neil Davidge

Don't be a - fraid,
Don't be a - shamed,

no,_____

op - en your mouth_____ and say,_____
to op - en your heart_____ and pray,_____

say what your soul   sings_____
say what your soul   sings_____

weather storm

Words & Music by Craig Armstrong, Robert Del Naja, Andrew Vowles, Grantley Marshall, Nellee Hooper, Cedric Napoleon, James Lloyd, Curtis Harmon & Cameron Murray

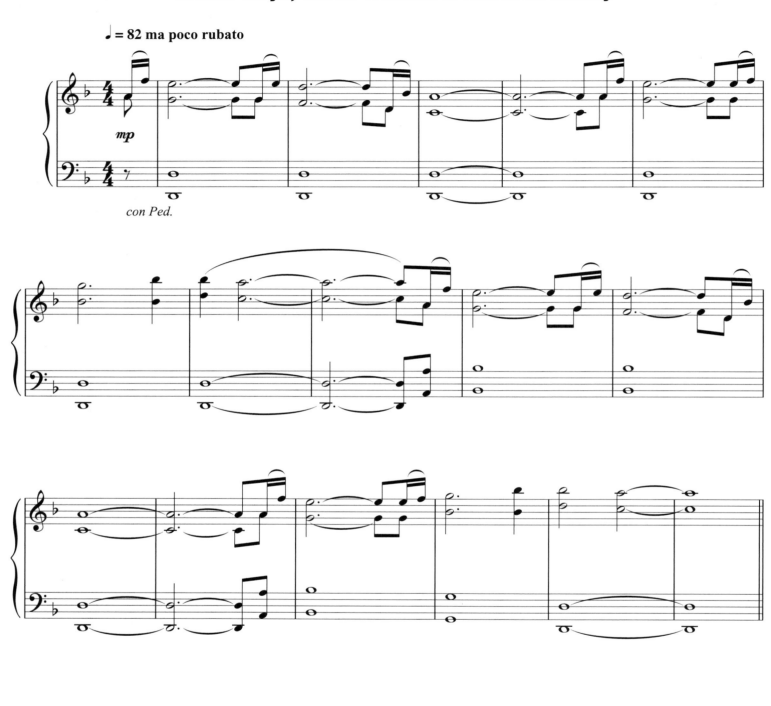

Quasi improvisato

espressivo

sim.

mp

Quasi improvisato

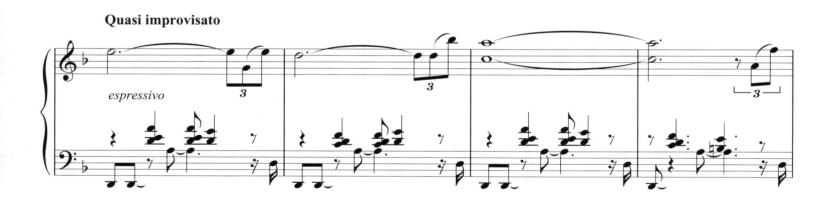

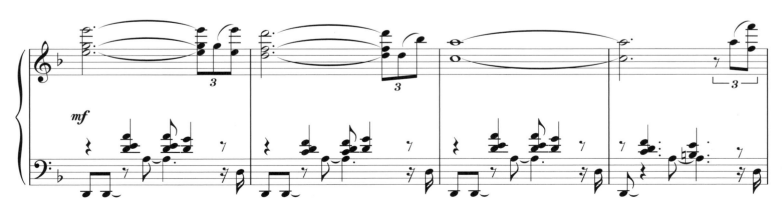

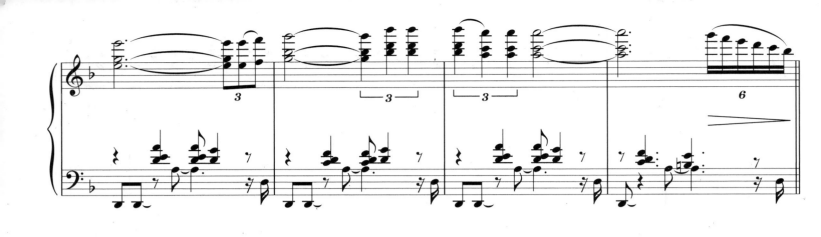

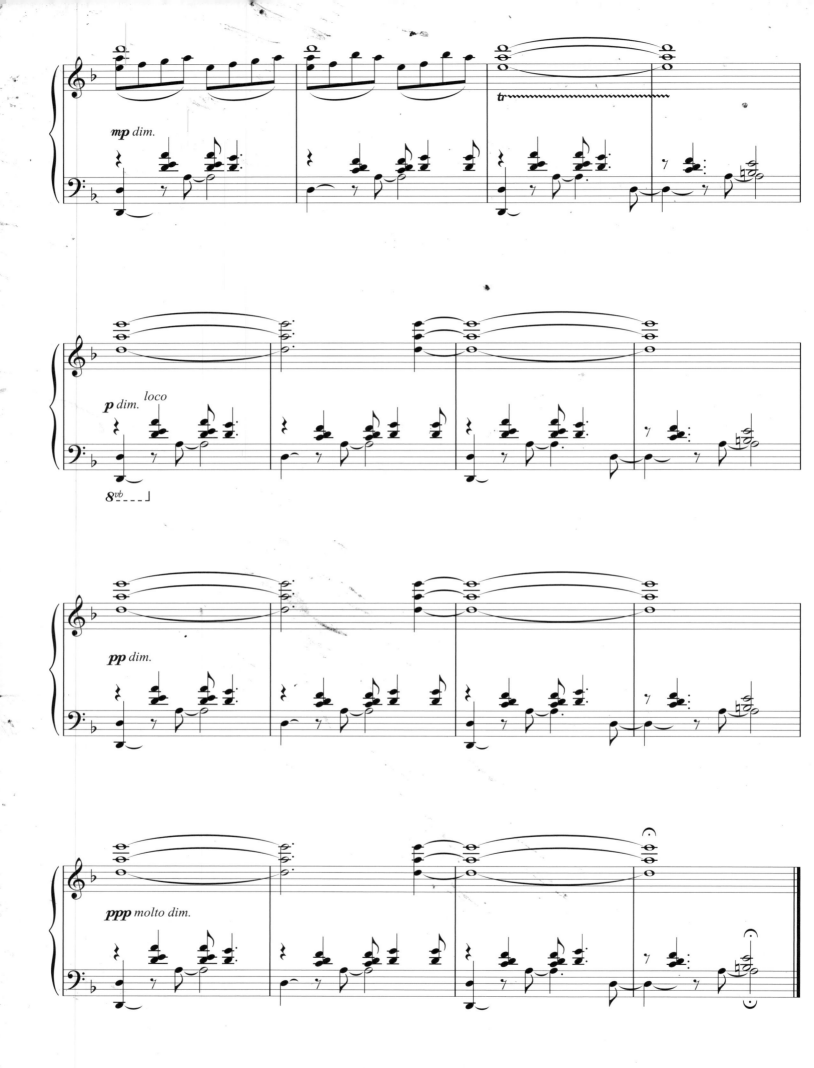